Original title:
The Grapefruit Glow

Copyright © 2025 Creative Arts Management OÜ
All rights reserved.

Author: Adrian Caldwell
ISBN HARDBACK: 978-1-80586-244-4
ISBN PAPERBACK: 978-1-80586-716-6

Vermilion Whispers

Bright bulbs teased the morning sun,
A citrus ball, oh what a pun!
With a wink, it rolled away,
Leaving laughter for us to play.

Squirrels danced in yellow cheer,
As juice dripped down without a fear.
They juggled peels with little flair,
While birds sang songs from up in air.

Golden Slices

On the table, slices shine,
Like little suns, oh how divine!
Friends gather near, they take a bite,
Squeals erupt, what a delight!

One slice slips, a comical fall,
Juice sprays high, a sticky squall.
Laughter thundered, hearts so light,
This golden fruit was pure delight.

Juicy Reverie

In a dream, we squeeze the fruit,
A fountain bursts, oh what a hoot!
Rubber ducks on a juice-filled tide,
Floating gently, oh, what a ride!

Dresses splashed in juice so bright,
While giggles echo through the night.
We slip and slide, it's all in fun,
Chasing sweetness, everyone!

Zesty Radiance

Zest here and there, oh what a show,
With citrus jokes, we steal the glow.
Each little seed, a punchline too,
Bouncing 'round like morning dew.

Squeeze the day, let laughter burst,
In the citrus world, we're all immersed.
Frogs in hats join in the jive,
With zesty smiles, we come alive!

Melodies of the Morning Dew

Morning fizz on my toasted bread,
Sipping juice, dreams in my head.
A citrus splash, oh what a tease,
Sticky fingers, buzzing bees.

Dancing droplets, the sun's bright cheek,
Lemonade giggles as we sneak.
With every sip, a silly twist,
Watch out for that citrus mist!

Ripe Moments Caught in Sunlight

Sun-kissed treasures hanging high,
Bouncing laughter as we try.
Chasing shadows, peeling skin,
Who knew fruit could make us grin?

Squirrels plotting, they're quite the jest,
Nuts and zest, they're on a quest.
Playful nibbling on sweet surprise,
Lemon zest twinkles in our eyes.

Lively Light in Ripened Bliss

Bright balloons of orange cheer,
Pinging laughter, drawing near.
Bubbles burst with every bite,
A fruity party, pure delight!

Juggling wedges, we take a chance,
Squeeze the juice, and watch us dance.
Slipping, sliding on the floor,
"Catch that zest!" – oh what a score!

Chasing Shadows of a Juicy Delight

Battle of flavors, who will win?
Zesty smiles, where to begin?
A game of puns, oh what a sight,
Citrus giggles, sheer delight.

Under the sun, we plot and plan,
With every bite, unleash the fun.
Jumps and jests till evening light,
In juicy laughter, we take flight!

Vibrant Swathes of Colorful Light

Beneath the sun, we chuckle bright,
A burst of shades, a zesty sight.
With every slice, the fun escalates,
A juicy party, oh, how it vibrates!

The laughter bursts with every taste,
Each twirl a joke, no need for haste.
Those citrus laughs, they dance and gleam,
In vibrant swathes, we sip and beam.

Luminous Citrus and Ocean Waves

At the shore, we splash and play,
In a sea of fruit, we float away.
Waves of laughter, with zesty flair,
The sun sings songs, we haven't a care.

Funny faces, a citrus cheer,
Each wave a giggle, we hold so dear.
From shimm'ring shores to skies so blue,
Luminous fun, just me and you!

The Sunrise in a Citrus Shell

Morning breaks with a burst of cheer,
A citrus hue, drawing us near.
We crack a grin, the day reveals,
In every peel, a laugh appeals.

The shell cracked open, sunlight beams,
In every slice, a dream, it seems.
With jokes and giggles, the day begins,
A fruity dawn, where laughter wins!

Blushing Citrus on the Horizon

Look out yonder, a blush in the sky,
Citrus smiles, floating high.
Witty banter in the morning mist,
Squeezing joy, who could resist?

As nightfall wraps with a dazzling glow,
Our giggles tumble, a fruity show.
With every hue, we sway and sway,
Blushing fun, to end the day!

A Dance of Light and Flavor

In the morning, a sunset's kiss,
A fruit so bright, you can't resist.
Juicy orbs in vibrant cheer,
Twirling zest, come dance near.

Slices shimmer, giggles grow,
With each bite, the laughter flows.
Not just a snack, a lively jest,
A citrus show that's simply best.

Puns on peels, in every hue,
Ticklish taste, we'll dine in zoo.
Flavor leaps, giggles abound,
In the orchard, joy is found.

Round and round, let's have some fun,
With each slice, another pun.
Orange laughter, lemon glee,
Come join this zestful spree!

Citrus Sunrise and Day's Awakening

A sunbeam sneaks through tangy scenes,
Bright and bold, like silly dreams.
Morning mist with citrus flair,
Juicy jests float in the air.

With each bite, a giggle grows,
Wakey-wakey! Here's how it goes.
Sour grin, sweet surprise,
Fruit-filled fun beneath the skies.

Zesty whispers, laughter loud,
In this breakfast, be so proud.
Orange slices, lemon zest,
Citrus breakfast is the best!

Cheesy smiles and citrus cheer,
Lemons laughing, oh so near.
Wake up your taste, join the spree,
This morning dance is wild and free!

Whispering Seeds of Citrus Lore

Once upon a fruit so bright,
Tales of citrus take their flight.
Seeds of laughter in the air,
Stories sweet beyond compare.

A peel like sunshine, warm embrace,
Cracking jokes at citrus pace.
Tales of trees, both tall and round,
The silliest fruit can be found.

Juicy rumors, bubbles burst,
Orange fairy tales, quench your thirst.
Underneath the leafy glee,
Zesty truths, come share with me!

Citrus secrets, laughter bright,
A world of flavor, pure delight.
Peel the layers, find the fun,
In every segment, laughter's spun.

Riddles Wrapped in Citrus Shells

What's bright and round, with a zingy grin?
A riddle wrapped, come take a spin!
Grapefruits giggle in morning's light,
Peeling back, a tasty sight.

What fits in hands, yet can't be tamed?
A twist of fun, you'll never be claimed.
Sour and sweet, a game of chance,
With every bite, you'll want to dance.

Can you taste the riddles inside?
Juicy puzzles, come take a ride!
In citrus land, where giggles reign,
Unwrapping joy, it's never plain.

Bites of sunshine, laughter bright,
Riddles waiting, pure delight.
With every slice, a new surprise,
Citrus jests, like butterflies!

Orchard's Warm Embrace

In a grove where shadows play,
Citrus smiles chase clouds away.
Oranges giggle, lemons tease,
Dancing joy upon the breeze.

Beneath the sun's bright, golden eye,
Lemonade dreams begin to fly.
A jester tree with fruits so round,
Tickles laughter from the ground.

The bees buzz tunes of silly rhyme,
As laughter loops like tangled twine.
Hang on tight, the harvest's near,
Who knew that fruit could bring such cheer?

With every bite, a zesty jest,
Nature's way to make us blessed.
In this grove of joy, we thrive,
Thank the fruit for being alive!

Twilight Citrus Serenade

As twilight drapes the orchard's floor,
Citrus scents invite us to explore.
A chorus of oranges starts to sing,
Melodies sweet as summer's fling.

Lemons dancing on evening air,
With silly hats, they haven't a care.
Juicy jokes in every slice,
Life's a punchline, oh so nice!

Grapefruit twirls, a graceful sway,
Wit and zing in bright array.
Sunset spills its golden cheer,
Fruit's funny tales are oh so clear.

With laughter echoing through the night,
Each citrus wink a burst of light.
In this orchard, under stars aglow,
We revel in the fruit's sweet show!

Luminous Peel

Peeling back the layers bright,
Each citrus twist a comical sight.
Luminous skin with a playful grin,
Sending chuckles from within.

Zesty zingers in every bite,
Banana jokes just don't feel right.
Oranges giggle, clementines snicker,
A juicy time that makes us quicker.

Puns are ripe and tangy too,
With every bite, there's more to do.
In this sunshine, we find delight,
Fruits can surely spark a light.

So let's toast to the citric fun,
With every laugh, we're on the run.
A luminous world of zest and flair,
Brings silly smiles everywhere!

Sunkissed Memories

Sunkissed skins and laughter bright,
In fruit-filled fields, the world feels right.
Grapes gossip while oranges sway,
Making sweet mischief every day.

A picnic spread with giggling treats,
Citrus slices, where humor meets.
Beneath the sun, our cares are few,
In juicy tales, we find our cue.

Chasing shadows, we take a bite,
Sunkissed laughter takes to flight.
Memories twinkle like stars above,
Each fruit a reminder of silly love.

As the day wraps in golden hue,
Nature's jest becomes our crew.
With a wink and a zesty cheer,
In every memory, the fruit is near!

Citrus Winks as Day Unfolds

Morning sun peeks in a cheeky way,
A zesty fruit is here to play.
With every slice, a smile appears,
Puns and giggles fill our ears.

Bright and bubbly, taste the tease,
Juicy laughter in the breeze.
Sour moments made so sweet,
Who knew breakfast could be a treat?

Rolling through the start of day,
Citrus antics lead the way.
Jokes and jests in every bite,
Colorful fun, oh what a sight!

Winks of zest dance on our plates,
With citrus sprinkles, life elates.
Juggling fruit, a silly show,
As laughter swells, we let it flow.

Glimmering Treats on Summer Days

Beneath the sun, a radresa glow,
Lemonade dreams, sweet and slow.
Laughter bubbles in the heat,
A citrus twirl on lazy feet.

Picnics spread with colors bright,
Cheeky fruits stealing the light.
Sipping drinks with silly straws,
Sticky fingers, endless applause!

Friends and laughter fill the air,
Zingy bites, a fruity dare.
Juicy chaos, oh what fun,
Sunkissed giggles on the run!

Endless summer, oh so grand,
With citrus treasures close at hand.
Every moment, pure delight,
Sunshine snacks, our hearts take flight.

Echoes of Sunshine in Each Slice

In every wedge a chuckle hides,
Bright and bold, let's ride the tides.
Sunshine giggles, zest on cue,
Each slice whispers something new.

Juicy tales and silly sprees,
With every bite, we feel the breeze.
Rind off laughter, it's a must,
Tasting joy, in citrus trust!

Bouncing ideas like fluffy clouds,
Jokes on fruit, we say it loud!
Echoes ring with merry cheer,
Slicing joy that we hold dear.

Our citrus kingdom, sweet and bold,
In every corner, laughter's gold.
Pulp and puns in every round,
On this playful, juicy ground.

Juiced Moments and Dappled Dreams

We toast to fun, our happy cups,
With winking fruit, and cheerful ups.
Sipping sweetness, oh so bright,
Chasing shadows, basking in light.

Zesty fables spin around,
In colorful hues, joy is found.
Twisting flavors, wild and free,
Each juicy sip, a giggling spree!

Messy smiles with sticky hands,
Witty banter, sunlit strands.
Moments shared, our laughter beams,
In fruity dreams, all is as it seems.

Sprinkled spritz on lazy days,
Cheeks aglow in citrus rays.
In every laugh, a tale entwined,
Surely, these treasures we won't mind.

A Symphony of Orange and Pink

In a bowl of sunlight bright,
Sits a fruit with such delight.
Peeling back its crazy skin,
Laughs and giggles all begin.

Juggling slices on a plate,
Flavor bursts we celebrate.
Each juice drop a little prank,
Sipping happiness, we tank!

A citrus song, we sing along,
Twirling taste in quirky throng.
In this dance of zesty cheer,
Who would guess it's fruit, oh dear?

Squirrels plot to steal a bite,
While we savor pure delight.
Orange blush with pinky streaks,
Citrus language, fruit still speaks.

Sweet Serenade of Citrus Smiles

Rolling in a fruit parade,
Zesty notes serenely played.
Juicy laughs that drip and flow,
Sweetest antics on the go.

Wobbly bowls of evening cheer,
Lemonade giggles, loud and clear.
Slicing wedges, oh so bright,
Dancing bubbles in the night.

With every zest, a chuckle grows,
Tasting joy as friendship sows.
Nature's candy, sunny rays,
A citrus dream that always stays.

Even fruit can laugh with ease,
As we munch on all that pleases.
Together, all the flavors twine,
In this slice of life, divine.

Coral Reflections at Daybreak

Morning quirks drape soft and bright,
Citrus dreams take joyful flight.
Pinks and oranges, skies aglow,
Ticklish flavors in a row.

Fruits in hats, a comical sight,
Dancing shadows, what a fright!
A breakfast jam that soon enthralls,
Lifting spirits with food balls.

Chasing rays like little sprites,
In this zesty day of bites.
Mirthful giggles in the breeze,
Fruitful moments aim to please.

Chopping fun, no time for gloom,
Citrus wonder fills the room.
With every slice, the laughter gleams,
Morning's juicy, fun-filled dreams.

The Orchard's Warm Caress

In the woods where sunshine plays,
Fruits conspire in joyful ways.
Colorful shapes hanging high,
Orchard mischief, oh me, oh my!

Laughter echoes through the leaves,
Silly tricks that joy retrieves.
Mischief managed, in a zest,
Tasting fun is truly best.

Squirrels giggle, birds all sing,
Love and laughter, that's the thing.
Juicy prizes, bright and bold,
A fruit story waiting to be told.

With every bite, we share our cheer,
In this orchard, love is near.
So come along, let's laugh and play,
With nature's gifts, let's seize the day!

The Glow of a Tangy Embrace

In the morning light so bright,
I took a sip, pure delight.
With a squirt right on my nose,
Zingy juice, where humor flows.

Bouncing back, I dripped with glee,
Such a splash, it's plain to see.
Friends all laugh, they can't ignore,
A tangy kiss, what's not to love more?

In a bowl where segments sit,
I pretend I'm a citrus wit.
Pillowy clouds of tangy zest,
Makes my breakfast feel the best.

So here we are with smiles wide,
Citrus giggles, none can hide.
With every bite, I sing and sway,
A silly start to my sunny day.

A Bouquet of Citrus Joy

In a garden rich with cheer,
Citrus fruits are drawing near.
Lemons laughing, limes in jest,
An orchard party—what a quest!

With a peel that shoots like darts,
Laughter sprouts in fruity parts.
Pineapples sporting hats so grand,
Citrus joy, let's take a stand.

With orange shirts and lemon ties,
We dance beneath bright sunny skies.
Smiles abound with every burst,
In this citrus hub, we all feel cursed!

"Watch me juggle!" calls a pear,
It slips and lands, oh how we stare!
We're a fruity, funny crew,
With a squeeze, our joy renew.

Melting Into Citrus Radiance

A bright slice fell off my plate,
What a mess! Such a fruity fate.
Juicy arms flung wide in play,
Hilarity wrapped in citrus sway.

The blender roars, a noisy beast,
Juice explodes, oh what a feast!
Sticky fingers, giggles abound,
In this messy joy, we're all spellbound.

With a zesty wink from lime,
We twist and turn, creating rhyme.
As the sun dips low at dusk,
Our laughter rises—oh, what a musk!

So together we will bask,
In this citrusy, juicy task.
Take a sip; let's light a spark,
Our funny crew ignites the dark.

Wave of Warmth in Juicy Realms

Oh, the sun shines on my face,
A juicy thrill, this happy place.
Sipping nectar, oh what bliss,
One little taste, you can't resist!

A wave flows through this tangy land,
With every bite, we'll make a stand.
Citron giggles, playful cheer,
In this sea of fruit, we persevere.

Limes roll in, they're on a spree,
What a sight, come dance with me!
Each droplet sings, it's quite the sight,
Our fruity friends bring sheer delight.

So raise your glass, let's toast today,
To the fun we've found in this spray.
In juicy realms, laughter soars,
With every sip, we want much more!

Bright Threads of a Tangy Tale

In a land where flavors play,
Colors dance and prance each day.
A zesty twist upon our tongues,
Where laughter's melody is sung.

Whimsical creatures made of zest,
In citrus costumes, they do their best.
Juggling rounds of vitamin C,
Making funny faces, oh can't you see?

A party in every juicy bite,
Turning gloom to sheer delight.
With puns so bad, they make you groan,
It's fruitastic fun, all on its own!

So grab a slice and laugh anew,
With every tangy twist, there's more to chew.
In this fruity world, we all are friends,
Where humor and flavor never end.

Soft Hues of Grapefruit Dreams

In pastel shades, the fruit does sleep,
Whispering secrets it cannot keep.
With a chuckle, it wakes each dawn,
Inviting joy with a mischievous yawn.

A pink hue giggles, bright and sweet,
As it swirls 'round in a citrus beat.
Dreamy flavors that tickle the nose,
Crafting laughter wherever it goes.

The forks and spoons start a joyful dance,
Chasing slices with a daring prance.
"Oh no!" cries the fruit, "Not my zest!"
But the fun just bubbles—it's truly the best!

So let's toast to tangy jest, dear friend,
With juicy laughter that'll never end.
A soft embrace from flavors bright,
In dreamy hues that spark delight.

Citrus Slices Beneath a Starry Sky

A picnic spread beneath the stars,
With citrus fruits and sweet candy bars.
We laughed aloud, as juice did splatter,
While wondering if the moon tastes better.

The pulpy surprise, a stardust tease,
We gather slices with such ease.
What's that? A dog with zest on his nose!
Oh, the tales that the fruit can compose!

Twirling under the night's delight,
Citrus giggles take to flight.
A joke about a lemon's grin,
Makes us laugh and dig right in!

The stars they wink, the night stays bright,
In the glow of citrus, all feels right.
With every citrus burst we proclaim,
Life's a funny, zesty game!

Dappled Glory of Citrus Fields

In fields of gold where smiles do grow,
The sun leaks laughter with a citrus glow.
Dappled with joy, the trees do sway,
As fruits of fun come out to play.

A squirrel in shades, wearing a grin,
Hiding behind a lime, trying to win.
"I'll share my stash, but only if you,
Can guess my age? Just one or two!"

The flavors unite, causing a ruckus,
As we pick and giggle, making a fuss.
With each quick pluck, we share a jest,
Leaving worries behind, feeling truly blessed.

Let's gather round, the harvest is here!
With jokes and zest, let's share the cheer.
In citrus fields where glory shows,
We find the funny in all that grows.

Mellow Citrus Clouds at Dusk

Beneath the skies of orange fluff,
Lemons giggle, feeling tough.
Limes swing with a wobbly grin,
Telling tales of how they spin.

Silly peels that twirl and dance,
The fruit parade takes a chance.
Count the segments, lose count quick,
Citrusy humor, quite the trick.

Juggling juice with zestful flair,
Citrons leap and cheer, beware!
The twilight sparkles with a dash,
Sour jokes that make you laugh.

Under the twilight's fruity kiss,
Grapefruits burst with citrus bliss.
Pineapples snicker at the vine,
Sunny delight, oh how they shine!

Ripening Radiance of Juicy Destinies

In orchards where the laughter flows,
A tangerine in striped clothes.
Peeling right in front of me,
An orange joke, just let it be.

Citrus charms are on the rise,
Bouncing high beneath the skies.
Grapples roll like merry fools,
Spreading joy like juice-filled pools.

Bananas peel their way to fun,
In a race, they say they won!
Kiwis giggle in delight,
Glowing bright in fading light.

Fruit's folly in this grand array,
As zestful laughter steals the day.
A squeeze of chuckles, vibrant tales,
Where every slice of joy prevails!

A Celebration of Citrus and Sun

Sunny days with zest in tow,
Citrus fruits in fun-time show.
The lemon curd's a cheeky treat,
With every tart and sweet repeat.

Lemony laughs and orange cheer,
Sipping sunshine, crystal clear.
Tart and sweet, they charm and quake,
In every bite, a funny flake.

Jollity in ripest hue,
Berry frolics, skies so blue.
A citrus conga, skip and hop,
This fruity carnival won't stop!

With puns and slices, laughter spills,
A citrus party that just kills.
Gather 'round, don't miss your turn,
The zest for life is what we learn!

Shimmering Reflections of Citrus Bliss

On the counter, gleams so bright,
Fruits are sparkling, what a sight!
A tangerine with style so fine,
Makes us giggle, oh divine!

Zesty wonders twirl around,
A marvelous, fruity playground.
Grapes whisper jokes in leafy shade,
While cheeky pears perform parade.

Sylph-like oranges prance with glee,
In a ballet, oh so free.
Their laughter echoes in the room,
As citrus aromas start to bloom.

Round and round, the fruit does spin,
Sipping sunshine once again.
With every peel, a joyous tune,
Gloriously bright under the moon!

Solar Fruit Serenade

In the garden where sunbeams dance,
A citrus ball takes a chance.
Wobbling on branches, looking so fine,
It's the star of the brunch, sipping sunshine.

With a wink and a twist, it rolls down the lane,
Bouncing and laughing in a fruity refrain.
Filling our bowls with zesty delight,
Who knew fruit could throw such a party so bright?

Marmalade dreams drip from above,
As bees buzz around, all in love.
It's the zest for life, so bright and bold,
Peeling back laughter, and stories retold.

With each juicy wedge, a giggle erupts,
In the kingdom of citrus where humor erupts.
Sun-kissed and cheeky, it's ready to shine,
All hail the fruit that's totally divine!

Crimson Essence

In the orchard where mischief brews,
Lies a fruit with a hue, that confuses the muse.
Bright and bold, it wears a grin,
Juicy conversations, where laughs begin.

A slice of this wonder, the prankster's delight,
Making tongues tingle, oh what a sight!
It's the life of the picnic, the hit of the day,
Keeping us giggling in the sun's warm sway.

One bite and it's laughter, it's sweet and it's tart,
Who knew that fruit could steal your heart?
Rolling on plates, with laughter galore,
Creating a scene that's hard to ignore.

As the juices flow, the jokes keep on springing,
This crimson essence is truly singing.
With friends gathered round, we relish the cheer,
In the land of the juicy, we'll never shed a tear!

Glimmering Citrus Fields

In fields of gold, where giggles sprout,
Citrus sprites frolic, what a shout!
Winking and blinking under the sun,
Each pearly orb knows how to have fun.

Glimmers of laughter dance on the breeze,
Tickling the senses with zesty tease.
Oranges appear with a chuckle and cheer,
Whispering secrets that only we hear.

Bouncing along, the fruit parade glows,
Their silly antics make us all pose.
With each juicy burst, we burst into song,
In the citrus fields, we all belong.

As the sun paints the sky in shades of delight,
We dance with the fruits, under stars bright.
Lemonade dreams are woven with glee,
In glimmering citrus fields, forever we'll be!

Sunset in a Slice

On a plate, a moment of joy does reside,
An orb of sunshine, with laughter inside.
With zest that can spark a giggle or cheer,
It's a slice of sunset, perfectly clear.

Each wedge tells a story, a rhyme in the glow,
A wink from the fruit, 'come take me, you know!'
Juices spill laughter, like summer rain,
As we savor each bite, our worries are slain.

In chortles and chuckles, we sip and we share,
Chasing down flavors that twist in the air.
Oh, the joy that it brings, in colors so bright,
This playful delight is our evening light.

As twilight descends on this citrus affair,
We raise our glasses, with laughter we share.
In slices of sunset, life's sweetness revealed,
Among friends and delight, our hearts are unsealed!

Sweet Illumination

In the kitchen, fruits are stacked,
A citrus joker, never lacked.
It rolls around, a nimble sprite,
Wakes the morning, such delight.

Peeling back that golden skin,
Juicy laughter tucked within.
Each segment bursts, a jovial cheer,
As breakfast giggles hover near.

A splash of color on the plate,
Each slice a prank that can't wait.
Oh, what a day to chase the gloom,
With tangy juice that fills the room.

Now watch it shine, a sly sunbeam,
Making every morning dream.
With every bite, joy starts to grow,
A fruity jest, what a show!

Aromatic Daybreak

Daylight breaks, the sun's a tease,
The air is fragrant, citrus breeze.
A round, bright ball of pure delight,
In the fridge, it shines so bright.

With a twist, a pop, the zest released,\nFlavor erupts, the laughter's increased.
It dances here, it wiggles there,
A bouncy breakfast in the air.

Each segment glows with playful humor,
Slides down the throat—an instant rumor.
With every bite, a silly grin,
Who knew breakfast could be a win?

So bring a spoon and join the fun,
With fruity puns, we've just begun.
Aroma wafts, let giggles flow,
As we sip the morning's glow!

Morning Zest

The day begins with quite a splash,
A zesty fruit in a tiny dash.
With every cut, the laughter bursts,
A citrus prank that never thirsts.

It winks at me from bowl so bright,
Its tangy laugh a pure delight.
With every slice, the day ignites,
In juicy joy, we find our flights.

I serve it up with silly flair,
A twist of lime tossed in the air.
The kitchen's buzzing, pots in rhyme,
As zest and giggles dance in time.

So lift your glass, let laughter flow,
In every sip, the fun will grow.
With morning zest, we start the show,
A brew of joy, a bright tableau!

Flavorful Elysium

In a land where flavors play,
A funny fruit leads the way.
With each bright bite, a jolly joke,
Happiness in every poke.

The sun laughs down from skies of blue,
As citrus spheres float into view.
With vibrant hues, they take the floor,
A joyful dance, forevermore.

Each burst of taste, a playful shout,
Making clouds of laughter sprout.
Oh, what a scene, so rich and bold,
A flavorful tale waiting to be told.

So gather round and share the cheer,
With fruity smiles spreading here.
In this Elysium, we all know,
Laughter sparkles in the glow!

A Tapestry of Yellow and Pink

In a bowl of morning cheer,
There sits a fruit so bright and dear.
It winks at me with zestful glee,
And giggles softly, 'Come, taste me!'

With each slice, juice starts to dance,
I take a bite—oh, what a chance!
The tangy pucker makes me grin,
As juice runs down my chin and skin.

I offer one to my cat nearby,
She sniffs and sneezes—oh my, oh my!
Not everyone's a fan, that's clear,
Yet laughter rings, we shed a tear.

Bright globes of fun in evening light,
They turn the mundane into a delight.
With every chuckle, my worries cease,
This citrus simply brings me peace.

Golden Moments in Citrus Light

A citrus sun begins to rise,
With sparkle and a hint of surprise.
Squeezed my troubles into juice,
And watched my worries slowly deuce.

Naked on a plate, they gleam,
I can't help it, I smile and beam.
A squirt of zest, oh what a prank!
That citrus burst!—Oh, how they stank!

Friends gather round to share the jest,
Entranced by fruits, they feel so blessed.
One guy's breath, a fruity blast,
We laugh till dinner's served at last.

As daylight fades, the laughter roars,
Citrus joy, we all adore.
In the warmth of the setting sun,
These golden moments, pure fun won.

Sweet Citrus Lullabies at Dusk

Underneath a twilight sky,
I slice a fruit, and oh my, oh my!
With each careful cut, I hum a tune,
Citrus serenades beneath the moon.

Each segment calls, a jolly song,
It beckons me to sing along.
A pinkish slice, a gleeful sight,
My taste buds dance in sheer delight.

A friend prances in with fruit in hand,
Declares a feast that's truly grand.
In laughter's arms, we toss the fruit,
And giggle as our plans take root.

With laughter bright, we say goodnight,
With citrus dreams to hold us tight.
Sweet lullabies in citrus haze,
Life's silly moments, we will praise.

Reflections on a Citrus Canvas

In a sunny kitchen, life's a show,
With slices set in vibrant row.
A canvas painted bright and bold,
Every slice a tale to be told.

A zestful artist with juicy flair,
Cracks jokes while handing citrus care.
The colors clash in a playful fight,
As giggles mix with morning light.

A sneak attack on taste buds reigns,
With laughter interlaced in chains.
A citrusy masterpiece unfolds,
As stories spill and laughter rolls.

With every bite, the canvas shines,
In our hearts forever binds.
Reflections frolic, whimsy sings,
In zesty joy, we find our wings.

Citrus Splashes in the Calm

In a fruit bowl, a splash occurs,
Lemon laughs with zestful purrs.
Orange rolls away with glee,
Chasing lime, oh can't you see?

Chorus of fruits in a merry dance,
Each one hoping for a chance.
Tangerines giggle, what a sight,
Their bubbly fun shines oh so bright.

A grapefruit tiptoes on the ledge,
Wobbling here, can't take the pledge.
"Let's all squeeze the day," it cries,
As they bounce beneath the skies.

Juice drips down like sunny rain,
Leaving behind a sticky stain.
But laughter rings in citrus air,
Who knew fruit could be so rare?

Citrus Kisses from Sunrise's Palms

Morning breaks with citrus cheer,
Oranges wink, the sun draws near.
Bananas slip, a silly jest,
They giggle loud, the day's a fest.

From the palms, fresh kisses fly,
Lime-winks sparkle, oh so sly.
With every peel, a laughter shared,
A fruit parade, we're all prepared.

In the hush, a pithy joke,
Tartness softens, sweetness spoke.
Cherry bites tease everyone,
Sour balls made the best of fun.

The laughter wakes the sleepy bees,
Inviting all to dance with ease.
Citrus dreams in dawn's embrace,
Orange kisses set the pace.

Glow of a Citrus Evening

Twilight brings a citrus show,
Peeling laughter, watch them glow.
A grapefruit winks, its cheeks so round,
Nighttime mischief all around.

Under stars, the fruits conspire,
Bouncing balls in bright attire.
Fishing for giggles, laughter flows,
In this patch where jocund grows.

The tangy zest of nighttime fun,
Candied laughter, everyone.
Lemon rolls into the pit,
"Who's next? It's time for wit!"

Silly shadows dance in light,
Oranges gleefully take flight.
In this glow, we all belong,
Citrus dreams, a jolly song.

The Warmth of Fruit Beyond Reach

Fruits aloft on branches sway,
Belly laughs heat up the day.
Plucking jokes from leafy trees,
Smiling fruits sway in the breeze.

Mango giggles, "Can you see?
I'm the juiciest of the spree!"
Pineapples tickle with their spines,
Jokes unfold in sunny lines.

With every bite, a chuckle springs,
Tartness sweet, the joy it brings.
A fruit fight in the warm embrace,
Citrus kids ran all the place.

But alas, the fruit's just out of reach,
With playful dreams, the trees do teach.
Underneath the orange stars,
Fruitful giggles dance on Mars.

Gentle Echoes of Juiced Happiness

In a world of zest and cheer,
Silly smiles in every sphere,
Peeling laughter, oh what fun,
Juicy jokes for everyone.

Squirrels sip on citrus drinks,
Tickled pink, they share their winks,
Oranges roll, a playful race,
Who knew fruit could have such grace?

The sun sets, the juice drips slow,
Belly laughs in the afterglow,
Citrus slices, quite a sight,
Squeezed in joy, oh what delight!

Dancing fruit in a happy jig,
Life's a smoothie, laugh big,
With every sip, a giggle flows,
In this squeeze, true happiness grows.

Petals of Citrus in Twilight's Glow

In twilight's blush, the fruit takes stage,
Petals twirl, like kids, uncaged,
Lemon hats and orange shoes,
Dance away, the night infuse.

Ripe mocktails in a funny twist,
Bananas join, you can't resist,
Lime cartwheels, pure joy's delight,
Citrus smiles shine, oh so bright.

As stars peek through the citrus haze,
The punchlines spark, in fruity ways,
Glowing skins underneath the moon,
Laughter, love in this soft tune.

Ponder not, just take a bite,
At twilight's end, all feels just right,
With every peel, a giggle sings,
In moonlit fun, the joy spring rings.

Essence of Citrus Cradled in Light

Sunkissed hues, a playful sight,
Citrus chuckles in warm light,
Juice drips down a comical lane,
Where every drop brings silly gain.

With zestful whispers in the breeze,
Mirthful moments come with ease,
Lemon laughter, oh what cheer,
Petty squabbles disappear.

Orange leaves in winding trails,
Funny fables, citrus tales,
Each slice reveals a punchy grin,
Cradled joy, let the fun begin!

So gather 'round, come one, come all,
In laughter's grasp, we can't fall,
The essence shared, a teasing sight,
In every glow, true love ignites.

Romantic Chapters of a Citrus Day

A morning breeze, with fruity dreams,
Awake in joy, or so it seems,
Banana boats on lemonade seas,
Crafting stories with silly ease.

In slices shared, a wink appears,
With every giggle, love endears,
Citrus kisses, tart and sweet,
In this chapter, hearts can beat.

Afternoons filled with funny games,
Oranges steer through wild flames,
Together we peel life away,
Dancing lightly through the day.

As night cascades, our laughter sways,
These joyful notes, our love displays,
In every chapter, laughter's play,
Romantic fruits hold sway today.

Radiating Bliss from Tree to Heart

In the orchard, laughter flies,
With yellow balls that meet our eyes.
They bounce around, a funny sight,
As sunlight dances, pure delight.

Bump into one, it's quite a thrill,
A zesty pop, an instant chill.
We giggle as the juice does spray,
Oh, what a silly, citrus day!

Slice a piece, oh what a mess,
Sticky fingers, we must confess.
We share our smiles and fruity bites,
In this wild fruit of sunny heights.

From the tree to heart, joy will flow,
Like a circus, a vibrant show.
So gather 'round, let worries cease,
In this orchard, we've found our peace.

The Essence of Warmth in Citrus

Peeling back the skin with flair,
A fruity burst will always share.
Its tangy charm, a piquant tease,
This sunshine snack brings us to knees.

The juice runs down our smiling chins,
A sticky game, oh, where it begins!
With every bite, a laugh will rise,
In citrus realms, we find surprise.

Dress it up in fanciful ways,
A citrus crown for sunny days.
With each nibble, silliness soars,
We revel in what nature pours!

So let the zest of life unfold,
With laughter bright and stories told.
Flavorful sunshine, pure and bold,
Golden moments, forever hold.

Fragrant Hues at Twilight's Edge

As day dips low, the colors blend,
In evening's joy, our laughter bends.
A burst of flavor fills the air,
Twilight's glow, a zesty affair.

We chase the breeze, a vibrant chase,
With juicy wonders in our space.
Twilight cocktails, silly spills,
A vibrant dance that gives us thrills.

In sunset's grasp, we make a toast,
To citrus dreams we love the most.
Fragrant hues and giggles shared,
In twilight's magic, none are spared.

So gather round, let joy ignite,
With fruity fun that feels just right.
In fragrant moments, we will glow,
Life's a party, don't you know?

Sunkissed Orbs in Life's Orchard

In life's grand orchard, we do find,
Sunkissed orbs, both sweet and blind.
Their laughter echoes in the breeze,
With every bite, our worries freeze.

Round and orange, bright as day,
They roll around, in curious play.
Aiming for the perfect catch,
Those funny fruits, they'll always hatch.

We wear them like a crown of glee,
A citrus circus, just you and me.
With every squirt, a giggle rings,
In the orchard, our joy takes wings.

So raise your glass to this delight,
With every sip, the mood is light.
Sunkissed orbs, forever fun,
In life's big orchard, we are one.

Citrus Spirit's Call

In the morning sun, I found my cheer,
A zesty fruit made my worries disappear.
With a smile so bright, it dances in light,
Sour and sweet, such a funny delight.

Lemon in a hat, orange with a grin,
Lime does a jig, let the breakfast begin!
Juicy laughter spills, in a glass or a bowl,
A citrus party, that's how we roll!

Peeling back layers, the pulp starts to show,
Squirting out juice, oh what a show!
A tangy explosion, I can't help but laugh,
This fruit's no drama, just a sunny half.

So join the fun, grab your citrus friend,
With each zesty bite, the giggles don't end.
Citrus spirit calls, in a world so whimsical,
Happiness served, in a way quite comical!

Juicy Tranquility

On a sunny day, I stroll to the stand,
Where fruits of joy in bright colors expand.
A tart little number, just waiting to play,
Bringing giggles and grins to the mundane day.

With one little slice, my troubles grow small,
A jolly fruit dance that will mesmerize all.
Caught in the groove, I can't help but sway,
In the joyful citrus ballet, I'll stay!

Zesty and sweet, what a silly affair,
Squirting out juice, I splatter everywhere!
With laughter on lips, and a grin ear-to-ear,
This juicy delight is no cause for fear.

A toast with a twist, cheers ring through the air,
Lifting spirits high, like balloons everywhere.
So here's to our peace, in this funny space,
Juicy tranquility, wrapped in its embrace!

Citrus Dreams and Dawn's Embrace

Wake up to sunshine, what a delightful sight,
An orange slice jumps into morning's light.
Dreams of citrus tang, oh what a tease,
With a wink and a smile, it was sure to please.

Pinkish pulp bursting, a flavor parade,
These sweet little segments, an edible charade.
Tasting the tang, I twirl and I spin,
In the world of fruit, we always win!

Banana took a trip, and got lost in the fun,
Joined by his buddy, a bright yellow sun.
Together they giggle, singing sweet songs,
As we munch on the fruits, nothing feels wrong.

So here's to the morning, bright and absurd,
With every juicy bite, my heart sings a word.
Citrus dreams come alive, on this beautiful place,
A dawn ripe with laughter, and bright fruity grace!

Sunlit Slices of Citrus Bliss

In the kitchen bright, under sun's warm kiss,
Lemon and lime cause a stir, pure bliss.
Slicing and dicing, what a silly sight,
Juicy gleeful chaos, oh, what a delight!

Tangerines giggle, in bowls stacked high,
Popping with laughter, as small snacks fly.
Each tart little taste, brings comedic cheer,
Fruit salad shenanigans, let's all gather near!

Peeling back laughter, zest sweetly spills,
Fresh fruity humor gives us all the thrills.
Kicking up flavors, oh let's have some fun,
With sunlit slices, our feast's just begun!

So lift up your forks, let's dance through the day,
One juicy morsel, taking blues away.
In a world full of joy, we can surely trust,
Citrus makes smiles, it's simply a must!

A Rhapsody of Citrus and Light

In the morning sun, they bounce and gleam,
Zesty rounds of joy, they dance and beam.
With a squirt and a laugh, they tease my tongue,
A laugh from the fridge, oh how they're hung!

Bright peels that giggle, so vibrant and bold,
Whispers of summer, their stories are told.
They roll off the counter, what fun to be had,
A citrus parade, it's hilariously mad!

Juicy little orbs with a wink in their skin,
In the fruit bowl saga, they always win.
Slicing them open releases a cheer,
"Juice is on the loose, bring it here!"

With every fresh bite, they brighten my day,
The tangy delight sends worries away.
So let's raise our cups, filled high to the brim,
To laughter and juice, to life's playful whim!

Citrus Hues Adrift in the Sky

Puffy clouds drift by, but look down below,
Citrus treasures scattered, a colorful show.
Lemonade rivers flow bright and carefree,
Sipping silliness, come laugh with me!

Up higher they swing, like balloons in the breeze,
Tangy and cheeky, they aim to please.
Lemon-lime giggles, my tongue does a dance,
Who knew citrus fruit could lead to romance?

In the zesty twilight, all colors collide,
Oranges in sunset, oh what a ride!
I trip on a peel, it's a slippery game,
With laughter in juice, it keeps me the same!

So let's toast our cups to this colorful flight,
Citrus adventures bring joy, pure delight.
With every bright slice, let humor unfurl,
In this fruity reverie, let's give it a twirl!

Tangy Reveries of Liquid Sunshine

A splash of bright color in every bite,
Liquid sunshine waits, what a tasty sight!
In jester hats made of zesty peel,
They giggle with glee; oh, what a meal!

Serve it up cold with a dash of delight,
Sippin' and slurpin', from morning to night.
A frothy umbrella atop this new drink,
Who knew tangy magic could teach us to wink?

Grapefruits in hats? Well, aren't they a show?
Juggling on counters, watch them go!
With each juicy gusher, they crack a big grin,
Citrusy humor, let the fun begin!

So gather your friends for this merry concoction,
In the world of citrus, we find our conviction.
Here's to laughter, to sunshine infused,
In the quirkiest feast, we'll never be snoozed!

Citrus Beacon of Hope at Dawn

As dawn breaks the night, there's a shimmer of gold,
Citrus contagion, a story unfolds.
Bright orbs of laughter greet me awake,
In breakfast delight, free spirits will quake!

With a giggle I slice, oh the jokes they will crack,
Squeezing out joy with no sign of lack.
The toaster pops up, and I burst into cheer,
Citrus companions will never bring fear!

Under the sun, oranges twirl with a wink,
Dance in the daylight, oh let them all drink!
They roll on the floor, what a juicy parade,
Where laughter erupts, the fun never fades!

So here's to the morn, with a zestful embrace,
In the heart of the fruit, find your own happy place.
Together we'll laugh, in this bright citrus run,
With each tasty moment, we'll bask in the fun!

Juicy Daydreams Under Golden Skies

In a garden where the laughter flows,
Round fruits shine like tiny suns that glow.
They bounce and giggle upon the vine,
Making all the worries seem just fine.

A squirrel in a hat, with shades so cool,
Claims the orchard as his summer school.
He'll teach you how to dance with zest,
And wear your fruit like a fancy fest.

The juice drips down like morning dew,
While cheeky birds sing their tunes so true.
Together we frolic, oh what a sight,
In this citrus world, everything feels right.

Every sip brings a grin, can you believe,
That life can be so sweet, oh please don't leave!
So let's toast to the days that never end,
With hairy fruits that are always a friend.

The Lightness of Citrus Joy

In a world where lemons wear a crown,
And capers leap up without a frown.
We throw a party on the kitchen slab,
And dance with joy while we fab and grab.

Oranges in pajamas, who would have guessed?
They twirl around feeling oh-so blessed.
With peels that slip and laughter spouts,
We bounce around as everyone shouts.

A parade of wedges with hats on tight,
They prance beneath the merry sunlight.
Watch out for the flying fruit parade,
As we all join in this zesty charade.

Sipping sunshine in a fizzy glass,
With giggles and jokes that never pass.
In this land of bright, where smiles flow,
We'll relish in the fun of each citrus show.

Morning's Delight in Zesty Splendor

The sun peeks up with a wink so sly,
As grapefruits giggle and start to fly.
With a jolt of zest, they spin and whirl,
While sleepy bees begin to twirl.

Marmalade tigers sneaking a taste,
Swirling around with no sign of haste.
They sip their breakfast, all orange cheer,
While giggling loudly, they spread good cheer.

Who knew that mornings could feel this bold?
With fruity antics, never growing old.
Juggling rinds like a circus clown,
In this juicy realm, we'll never frown.

With each burst of flavor, we lift our voice,
For around us, the sun makes us rejoice.
So grab a slice of this morning brew,
And let your spirits soar and stew.

Nectar at Dawn's First Breath

As dawn arrives with a zesty tease,
Fruits awaken with the softest breeze.
Honey bees buzz in a playful whirl,
While sweet nectar drips, spinning round and twirl.

Pineapple pickles in a fancy hat,
Saunter around, oh imagine that!
Lemons play hopscotch with strawberry mates,
Creating a chorus that celebrates states.

Laughing so hard, a peach can't hold on,
It rolls down the hill at the break of dawn.
Let's catch this moment, share a big laugh,
With fruity delights, we'll craft a sweet craft.

Here's to the nectar that fills the air,
With each spoonful, joy is hard to compare.
So lift your glass, let's chug with glee,
In this quirky feast, you're wild and free.

Tangy Luminescence

In a bowl sat the fruit, so bright,
It winked at me, a comical sight.
I peeled it back, what a big surprise,
It burst like laughter, oh my, oh my!

Each slice like a joke, fresh and zesty,
A citrus giggle, can't help but be testy.
I pucker and grin, my mouth on a spree,
Laughing with juices that dance wild and free.

Those tangy spots, they hide in my grin,
Every bite a chuckle, where do I begin?
I share with my friends, they all get a taste,
Together we giggle, no smile goes to waste.

So here's to the fruit, that brings such delight,
In every bright orb, there's joy, pure and right.
With each funny bite, and laughter to share,
We savor the glow, life's silly affair.

Harvest of Light

From the tree, they dangle, a brilliant show,
Funny little orbs, dressed to glow.
I reach for one, it rolls with a grin,
A wobbly jester, let the fun begin!

Clouds gather 'round, they laugh and they tease,
As I chase the sun with a clumsy breeze.
One slips and splats, oh what a sight!
A citrus riot in the warm sunlight.

We gather 'round with splashes of cheer,
Slurping up sunlight and giggles sincere.
Each bite a comet, racing through air,
Tickling our tongues with fruity flair.

So let's toast to the harvest, with sass and with zest,
In a world so bright, we're truly blessed.
With smiles like fruit, we join in the fun,
In the glorious field where laughter's begun.

Pulses of Sunlight

In the morning light, they look so divine,
Round and cheerful, they're fruit with a shine.
I crack one open, what a juicy blast,
Like laughter exploding, a giggle unsurpassed.

Each morsel a bounce, a jest to behold,
As friends join in, and the tales unfold.
A splash of tangy, a tickle on taste,
We race to devour, no moment to waste.

The kitchen's a circus, a fruity delight,
With zest in our jokes, we're all quite a sight.
We juggle the segments, oh what a game,
With each little splash, we're never the same!

So here's to the fruit, in bursts of bright fun,
Pulses of sunlight, for everyone!
With every sweet squirt, let laughter erupt,
Together we munch, in joy we're swept up.

Coral Skies

Glistening gently, like coral afloat,
A splash of the sun, in a fruity boat.
The rinds hold secrets, the smiles inside,
Each bite a giggle, a flavorful ride.

We slice through the evening, sweet laughter bursts,
As juices collide, quenching silly thirsts.
A blush on our cheeks, from laughter and fruit,
In this coral glow, we're all resolute.

A pratfall or two as we play and we munch,
With laughter our dessert, we savor the crunch.
The sunset's a canvas, we paint with our cheers,
As citrusy joy wipes away all our fears.

So here's to the skies, where humor ignites,
In the bountiful harvest of silly delights.
With bright coral shades and a fruity embrace,
We dance in the glow of this happy place.

Citrus Glow

Underneath the tree, a deck of orange cards,
With jokers aplenty, we'll play like goofballs.
Peeling back laughs, like a playful surprise,
The sweetness of zest, how the fun quickly flies.

A splash in the air, like tricks at a show,
Every slice takes a bow, what a bright glow!
We juggle our snacks, with giggles galore,
In the silly dance, we beg for more.

The juices are rockets, igniting our glee,
As we burst out laughing, so wild and so free.
With sunshine and humor wrapped in a bite,
Our sweetest adventures, they feel just right.

So raise up your fruit, let the fun overflow,
In this zesty celebration, we bask in the glow.
With each playful moment, beneath this blue sky,
We savor the laughter, and let our joys fly.

Citrus Dawn

Morning light spills, a zesty tease,
Chasing away dreams with a tangy breeze.
Oranges giggle, lemons sing a tune,
As the sun rises, making fruit swoon.

Peels in a pile, a citrus parade,
Mandarins bouncing, no plans to fade.
Limes do the limbo, what a sight to see,
Juicy confetti, oh, what glee!

Breakfast awaits, a salad of zest,
Who knew fruit parties could be the best?
With each juicy bite, laughter spills wide,
In this citrus fiesta, we all take pride.

Sunshine fills glasses, squeeze and serve,
A toast to the fruit that we all deserve.
With giggling oranges, and lemons in tow,
We dance in the light of the citrus glow.

Fragrant Ember

A funky fruit salad, what a delight,
Slicing and dicing, let's take flight.
Rinds in the air, zest on the floor,
Smiles shared sweetly, who could ask for more?

Pineapples wear hats in this fruity spree,
While grapefruits gossip, sipping iced tea.
Cherries are blushing, in their red attire,
While strawberries chat with a dash of fire.

Dancing in dishes, they jive on the spoon,
With each citrus laugh beneath the bright moon.
Fruity friendships bloom with each sticky bite,
In this fragrant ruckus, everything feels right.

Scent of the orchard, laughter afloat,
Fruit salad sings with each zesty note.
Oh, savor the parts that make you feel young,
Join the fruit party, let joy be sung!

Radiant Citrus Dreams

In the land of citrus, where laughter grows,
Tangerines waltz, as silliness flows.
Magic in marmalade, oh so sweet,
Where grapefruits giggle, and zest joins the beat.

A lemony prank, they squeeze and they squirt,
A splash on your face, oh what a flirt!
The oranges roll, in a jolly parade,
While limes throw confetti, their joy unafraid.

Minty green cousins swoop down and join,
In this tangled orchard, the fun's never gone.
Cherries pop out from behind fruity walls,
As laughter erupts through the citrus halls.

With smiles abundant, and crunches so bright,
Each vibrant fruit brings pure sheer delight.
So, grab a slice, let the fun explode,
In this radiant dream, let happiness flow.

Sun-Kissed Nectar

A nectar so sweet, it glows like the sun,
With fruit all around, the journey's begun.
Peeling the laughter, a citrus confetti,
Where zesty jokes are always plenty.

Watermelons wiggle, while lemons perform,
With oranges' chuckles, the vibe is warm.
Juices collide in a wild fruit dance,
As cherries twirl round in a joyful trance.

Sunshine in bottles, we sip and we share,
With giggly grapefruits, who really would care?
Life's too short for a mundane routine,
So let's sip on sunshine, and live like a dream!

Gather the crew for a zesty retreat,
In this sun-kissed moment, we all feel complete.
Let laughter and sweetness, together ignite,
In this fruity adventure, we'll dance through the night!

Radiant Orbs of Morning Light

In the garden, orbs do shine,
They bounce with laughter, oh so fine.
With a wink, they roll away,
Chasing shadows, they love to play.

Sunbeams giggle, bright and bold,
Each one tells a tale of old.
Dance around the morning dew,
What funny friends these orbs pursue!

With peels so bright, they try to tease,
Juggling rays like buzzing bees.
Holding jokes, each ripeness beams,
In the daylight, joy redeems.

But when the night begins to fall,
They snicker, "More light! Who'll call?"
With smiles wide and zestful cheer,
Their radiant laughter fills the sphere.

Zestful Whispers in the Breeze

Whispering winds tell silly tales,
Of fruity dreams and gusty gales.
Wobbling down the winding lane,
A citrus jest, quite insane!

The breeze gives fruit a cheeky nudge,
They bounce and giggle, never budge.
"Let's play tag!" they chirp with glee,
As they race 'neath a waving tree.

With zestful notes, they sway along,
Crafting tunes like a silly song.
A fruity party in full swing,
Nature's laughter is the thing!

In playful hues, they swirl around,
Creating joy that knows no bound.
With a wink and a joyful grin,
In this fruity world, we win!

Juicy Hues Beneath the Sky

Beneath the sky, what colors gleam,
Round and vibrant, like a dream.
They bask in rays, no time to waste,
Life's a juicy, zest-filled taste!

With every squirt, a splash of fun,
They giggle bright when day is done.
"Catch us quick!" they tease and roll,
A circus act, they're on a stroll!

Hues like laughter paint the air,
Colorful stories everywhere.
With twists and turns, they never mind,
In juicy shades, joy we find.

Each drop of humor, sweet and bold,
Jubilant secrets to unfold.
Underneath the shimmering glow,
This fruity world, a grand tableau!

Fragrant Sunrise Over Citrus Groves

As dawn awakes with a fragrant cheer,
Citrus dreams start to appear.
Songs of zing float in the air,
Fruitful laughter without a care.

Little orbs in quiet rows,
Chasing rays as bright hope grows.
With each breath, they share their zest,
Smiling wide, they're truly blessed.

A morning dance of hues and peels,
Jumbling joy, the fruit reveals.
With silly giggles, they embrace,
Golden warmth in every place.

The sunrise grins, it joins the fun,
In citrus lands, we are all one.
With laughter lining every grove,
This playful place is what we love!

www.ingramcontent.com/pod-product-compliance
Lightning Source LLC
Chambersburg PA
CBHW070315120526
44590CB00017B/2684